Heinemann
InfoSearch

A Band of Gorillas

Heinemann Library
Chicago, Illinois

Richard and Louise Spilsbury

Originated by Dot Gradations Ltd
Printed in Hong Kong, China by Wing
  King Tong

08 07 06 05 04
10 9 8 7 6 5 4 3 2 1

Library of Congress Cataloging-in-Publication Data
Spilsbury, Louise.
  A band of gorillas / Louise and Richard Spilsbury.
    p. cm. -- (Animal groups)
Summary: Describes the physical characteristics,
behavior, habitat, and group life of gorillas.
Includes bibliographical references and index.
  ISBN 1-4034-4687-3 (HC lib. bdg.) 1-4034-5413-2 (PB)
  1. Gorilla--Juvenile literature. [1. Gorilla.] I. Spilsbury,
Richard,
1963- II. Title. III. Series.
  QL737.P96S64 2004
  599.884--dc21
                            2003010351

Acknowledgments
The author and publishers are grateful to the following
for permission to reproduce copyright material:

p. 4 NHPA/Daniel Heuclin; pp. 5, 11, 17 OSF/Konrad
Wothe; pp. 6, 8, 10, 15 NPL/Bruce Davidson; p. 7
OSF/Andrew Pluptre; pp. 9, 12, 14, 18, 22, 26
NHPA/Martin Harvey; p. 13 NPL/Karl Amman; p. 16
Corbis/SYGMA/Forestier Yves; p. 19 Ardea/Adrian
Warren; p. 20 OSF/Stan Osolinski; p. 21 Corbis/Tom
Brakefield; p. 21 OSF/Daniel Cox; p. 23 Corbis/Yann
Arthus-Bertrand; pp. 24, 25 National Geographic; p. 27
OSF/Martin Colbeck; p. 28 FLPA/Silvestris.

Cover photograph of a band of gorillas reproduced with
permission of NHPA/Martin Harvey.

Every effort has been made to contact copyright
holders of any material reproduced in this book. Any
omissions will be rectified in subsequent printings if
notice is given to the publisher.

Contents

Some words are shown in bold, **like this.** You can find out what they mean by looking in the glossary.

What Are Gorillas?

Gorillas are the largest **apes** in the world. They are very similar to humans. Gorillas have two legs and two arms and can be as tall as a human when standing. They have ten fingers and ten toes, and small ears on each side of their head. Gorillas even see, hear, and smell in much the same ways as people do.

What are apes?

Apes are very intelligent and are the animals that are most closely related to humans. Gorillas, gibbons, chimpanzees, and orangutans are kinds of apes. Monkeys are not apes. The main difference between apes and monkeys is that apes have no tail that you can see, and they have toes that can grip.

Gorillas have black or brown hair on most of their body. They do not have hair on their face, chest, palms of their hands, or soles of their feet. Their arms are long and **muscular** and their legs are fairly short.

Do males and female gorillas look alike?

Male gorillas can be twice as large as the **females.** Large adult male gorillas weigh up to 550 pounds (250 kilograms), which is more than the combined weight of three adult humans! Males and females look different in other ways, too. Males have sharp **canine** teeth and a raised lump on the top of their head. The hair on a male's back starts to turn silvery-gray after about ten years. This is why older males are known as **silverbacks.**

Do gorillas live in groups?

Each gorilla is an individual that spends some of its time alone, but all gorillas are **social** animals. This means they live together in groups. A group of gorillas is called a band. In this book we look at some of the typical ways a band of gorillas lives and behaves.

Individual gorillas look different and have different skills, just like humans. And, like humans, most gorillas live together in groups.

What Is a Gorilla Band?

Most bands of gorillas have between 5 and 10 members, but they can contain up to 30. A typical gorilla band is made up of one adult **silverback male**, one or two young adult males who still have black hair on their backs, three adult **females**, and two or three youngsters.

Gorillas do most things together with their band.

What do gorilla bands do?

A band's day usually starts just after sunrise. The gorillas head off in search of food then eat for several hours. By midday, it is time for an afternoon nap. The gorillas rest for four to six hours. In the late afternoon the band sets off to feed again until early evening. When the sun sets, they settle down for a good night's sleep.

Who leads a band of gorillas?

The biggest and strongest adult male leads a band of gorillas. This silverback is the **dominant** member of the band. He decides what the band members will do each day, such as where and what they eat. He sorts out arguments in the group, and he also defends the females and the youngest gorillas against danger.

The silverback does not have one female partner. He **mates** with all the adult females in his band. They are the mothers of the other gorillas in the group, and he is the father of all of them.

The silverback is at the center of life in a band of gorillas. When he moves to another place, the whole group moves. When he stops to rest, the other gorillas in the band stop to rest, too.

Who's who in a gorilla band?

The **dominant** female is the one the **silverback** has known the longest. She has a higher **rank**, or importance, than the silverback's other partners. The more important a female is, the closer she can stay to the silverback. It is good to be close to the silverback because he is the group's protector. If another animal threatens her or her young, the silverback chases it away.

Who grooms who?

Grooming is when one animal cleans another's hair and skin. Who you groom depends on who's who in the group. Females in a band do not groom each other, but they often argue over who gets to groom the silverback because each of them wants to win his favor.

The silverback shows his dominance in different ways. He might stare or frown to stop an argument between females. He sometimes struts around, like this, to show he is boss.

Grooming is an important part of the gorilla band's life. Young gorillas get the most grooming from their mothers, whether they like it or not!

Where Do Gorillas Live?

Gorillas live in Africa in forest **habitats** of some kind. They live in two different areas in Africa. Most live in lowland **rainforests**, and the rest live higher up in mountain areas.

Lowland gorillas

Lowland gorillas live on land that is low and not hilly. They live in rainforests, where it rains almost every day and the trees grow very tall. There are two groups of lowland gorillas. Western lowland gorillas live in western Africa in parts of Cameroon, the Republic of Congo, the Central African Republic, and Gabon. Eastern lowland gorillas live in the eastern lowlands of the Democratic Republic of Congo.

Many bands of lowland gorillas gather at swampy forest clearings like this called bais (you say "byes"). There are many bais across central Africa.

What is a home range?

A **home range** is the area that a gorilla band lives or travels in. It has to be big enough to supply the band with all the food they need. Most gorilla home ranges cover an area of between 3 and 25 square miles (5 to 40 square kilometers). The **silverback** chooses the group's home range. Bands of gorillas may have home ranges that overlap each other, but they usually keep out of each other's way.

Mountain gorillas

Mountain gorillas live in high mountain forests in just two places in central Africa. Some live in southwestern Uganda, and the rest live in the Virunga mountain range between Uganda, the Democratic Republic of Congo, and Rwanda.

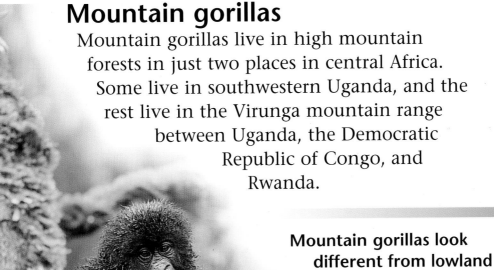

Mountain gorillas look different from lowland gorillas. Adults are bigger, their nose is a different shape, and they have longer hair. Their hair helps keep them warm in the cold mountains.

11

How Do Gorillas Get Around?

Gorillas do not stay in one place for very long. Each morning they move on to find new places to eat. They travel over half a mile (about 1 kilometer) around the **home range** each day, but they may have to travel farther in places where there is less food.

Gorillas usually walk on all fours. Their front arms are especially long and strong and they walk on the knuckles of their front hands. This is called knuckle walking. Gorillas also can climb trees to get food. They use their strong front arms to help them climb. Larger gorillas climb less than young gorillas because they are so heavy they would break thin branches!

Gorillas walk on their knuckles, like this, when they are on the move. They can walk upright—on their two back legs—but they usually only do this for a few steps.

Where Do Gorilla Bands Sleep?

Every evening, when it is time to sleep, gorillas make a new nest to sleep in. Each gorilla builds its own nest, except youngsters under three years old, who get to sleep with their mother in her nest. Gorillas make a nest by sitting in a good spot among lots of leafy plants or branches. Then they bend and pull down branches and leaves and tuck them in under and around themselves to form a comfy bed.

Most young gorillas make their nests in trees. **Females** may nest on the ground or in trees. Adult **males** usually nest on the ground because they are so heavy the branches may not hold their weight. Gorillas also make nests for resting in during the day.

Gorillas always make nighttime nests within the band's home range, but they are in a different place each night because the band wanders around to a different part of their range during the day.

What Do Gorillas Eat?

Gorillas are **herbivores**—they eat mainly plants. The kinds of plants a gorilla band eats depends on where it lives. Mountain gorillas feed mainly on green plant parts like leaves. They eat around 40 different kinds of plants, including vine, thistle, and wild celery. Lowland gorillas have a wider choice of food plants in the **rainforest.** They eat the leaves, **pith**, roots, and fruits of around 200 different plants, including ginger.

Gorillas sometimes eat tiny animals such as worms, ants, and **termites**, if they find them. Mountain gorillas also eat some soil. Scientists think they do this because soil contains **minerals** they cannot get from plants. Gorillas get most of the water they need from the morning dew on leaves that they eat and from the plants they eat, which contain water.

Gorillas choose to eat plant parts they like, such as the pith inside a stem, and leave the rest. This leaves the plant healthy so it will keep growing and provide them with more food later.

Finding and preparing food

The **silverback** tries to find food sites where there is enough for the entire band to eat. Adult gorillas usually sit apart from each other while feeding, but move closer if there are only a few food plants in an area. If there is only one treat, such as some ripe bananas available, the silverback often pulls **rank** and takes them for himself!

Gorillas use their fingers to collect and prepare food—often peeling leaves off a stem. Like humans, they can press their thumb against a finger to pick up small things.

Do gorillas eat a lot?

Gorillas are large animals, so they have to eat a lot of plants to get all the **nutrients** they need. Gorillas spend about a third of their day eating, and adult **males** can get through about 65 pounds (30 kilograms) of food each day—that is about the same weight as a bale of hay!

How Do Gorillas Care for Their Young?

A **female** gorilla is ready to have her first baby when she is between seven and ten years old. **Males** become **silverbacks** between nine and thirteen years old and can **mate** with a female then, if they have their own band. Gorillas can have babies in any season of the year.

After a male gorilla and a female gorilla have mated, a baby gorilla grows inside its mother for around eight to nine months before it is born. Females usually have one baby at a time. Some have been known to have twins, but this is not common. Newborn gorillas weigh about 4 pounds (2 kilograms). Like all **mammals**, they feed by **suckling** milk from their mothers. They suckle until they are about two years old.

A newborn gorilla is helpless and needs constant attention. Its mother carries it close to her belly until it can cling on to her tummy hair by itself. Gorilla babies have pink or light gray skin, but their skin turns dark by the time they are about one and a half months old.

Growing up

The huge silverback is a caring father who plays with his baby once it starts to crawl around at eight weeks old. Babies stay close to their mothers at this stage, but after three months they begin to explore farther away from their parents. At this age, they also ride on their mother's back instead of her front and make different sounds. By six months old, young gorillas start to climb trees, too.

Baby gorillas soon start to travel on their mother's back, although they are able to walk at about four to six months of age. They are carried up to about two years old. Then the young gorillas walk by themselves all the time and start to spend long periods near their father.

How do young gorillas learn?

Young gorillas learn all they need to from the adults in their band. All gorillas help to look after the youngsters as they grow. Adults share food with them, carry them, cuddle and **groom** them, take naps with them, and play with them.

17

How Do Gorillas Relax?

Gorillas relax around the middle of the day. This is the time when all the gorillas get together and rest as a band. It is also the time when the young gorillas can play together, while the adults sit around.

Most of the adults gather around the **silverback** and doze. Sometimes they make day nests to rest in, which are usually quite close together. Some of the gorillas spend time cuddling and **grooming** each other. When gorillas groom they help keep each other healthy, but grooming is also a friendly thing to do. It makes the gorillas in a band feel closer to each other and more like a team.

Gorillas spend about a third of their waking hours resting and relaxing. They use this time to **digest** their leafy meals. This relaxation time is also very important for the **social** life of the band.

How do gorillas play?

When young gorillas play, they wrestle and play games such as follow the leader or chase. Sometimes the adults join in and play with the youngsters. Gorillas even play with things that they find. People have seen them catch frogs and lizards, and stroke and play with them like pets before letting them go!

Why do young gorillas play?

Gorillas play for fun and for other reasons. As they play with each other, they get to know everyone in the band. This helps them get accepted as part of the group. When youngsters play, they are also learning to **communicate** with each other.

A favorite game of most young gorillas is play-fighting. They toss each other around, grunting and laughing as they play.

Do Gorillas Talk to Each Other?

Animals that live in a group need to be able to tell each other things. They need to **communicate.** Gorillas mostly communicate using sounds and face or body movements. Gorillas make around twenty different sounds. They can grunt, howl, scream, bark, hoot, and roar. Each sound has a different meaning. For example, **silverbacks** bark to warn the band of danger, and youngsters whine if they think they are going to be left behind.

Gorillas also use body movements to tell each other things. For example, when one gorilla crouches low and approaches another from the side, it is saying it knows the other gorilla is **dominant.**

When a silverback beats on his chest, like this, it makes a very loud noise that tells everyone he is the boss.

Gorillas can show how they are feeling—whether they are happy, sad, or scared—using their faces. Just as humans do.

Male gorillas make most of the noise in a band.

Does a Band Ever Change?

Gorilla bands change when young gorillas grow up and leave to have a family of their own. **Females** usually leave when they are about eight years old. They often join a young **male silverback** from a different group and start a new band with him. Some join a silverback that already has a band. Females choose a silverback that is big and strong and has a good **home range**.

When do young males leave a band?

Males usually leave their family band at around eleven years old. Some try to take over another silverback's band, but at age eleven most are not strong enough to defeat an older male. Most young silverbacks spend a few years living alone after they leave the band they were born in.

In a band, a female's **rank** follows the order in which she joined the band. Most young females try to join a male who is alone, so they become number one in their band.

How do new bands form?

Young adult males spend the years they are alone finding a home range of their own. When a lone gorilla is about fifteen years old, he is big and strong. Now he should be able to find a female that is willing to begin a new band with him.

What happens when a silverback gets old?

Sometimes, when a silverback is old and weak, a younger silverback may be able to take over his band. The older silverback leaves the band and lives alone until he dies. If a silverback dies suddenly while he still leads a band, the group may fall apart. The adult females in a band are not related and the silverback is the only link between them.

When a young male first leaves his family group, he stays nearby for several months. Then he leaves completely to find a home range of his own.

23

Do Gorillas Fight?

The gorillas in a band usually live together peacefully, although, like people, they sometimes argue. Gorillas in the same band may disagree about nest sites or who should **groom** the **silverback.** Silverbacks resolve arguments within a band by grunting to tell the other gorillas what to do.

A silverback intruder

A silverback leader is less gentle with other silverbacks that approach a band because they may want to take over his group. The two silverbacks do not fight right away. First the leader of the band tries to scare the intruder away. He stands on his back legs, beats his chest with cupped hands, and screams or roars. Then he runs around on all fours and beats the ground with his hands.

When an adult silverback tries to scare off an intruder, he may throw twigs in the air as he roars. He may also release a strong smell of sweat to make sure everyone notices him. This silverback is thrashing around in a pool of water.

The silverback's noisy **display** is often enough to chase away a young adult **male**. If the intruder persists, the silverback may charge toward him on all fours. He usually does not charge right into the intruder, but instead runs past him. This show of power is usually enough to get rid of the other gorilla without a fight that would risk both silverbacks getting injured.

What happens when gorillas fight? • • • • • • • • • • • • • • •

If the silverback's displays are not enough to frighten off another silverback, a real fight begins. A fight can continue on and off for several days and can be quite vicious. Gorillas use all their strength and their sharp teeth. **Females** and young adult males in the band may join in, too, and can get injured.

In most of the fights that happen between silverbacks, the larger male wins.

Leopards occasionally catch and eat smaller gorillas, but adult gorillas have no wild **predators.** Their only enemies are people. Because of hunting and the destruction of **rainforests,** there are far fewer gorillas today than there were in the past. There is a real danger that these magnificent animals may become **extinct.**

This **ranger** has found a trap that has been set by hunters. Traps like these kill many gorillas every year.

How many babies?

Female gorillas do not have many babies in a lifetime. Most have their first baby at ten years old and have one baby at a time, every three to four years. Many of the babies die before their first birthday. Wild gorillas live for between 30 and 35 years, so each female only has about four healthy babies in her lifetime. This means that gorilla numbers cannot increase quickly when they drop low.

Why are rainforests being destroyed?

People chop down the forests where gorillas live to use the wood for fires and to clear the land for farms or houses and other buildings. Large logging companies also cut down trees to sell the wood for timber to make houses and furniture.

Why do people hunt gorillas?

Some hunters and **loggers** kill gorillas for their meat, which is also sold in grocery stores and restaurants. Some farmers kill gorillas so they will not eat from their fields near the edge of the forest. Sometimes gorillas are injured or killed if they stumble into traps set for other animals. People also capture gorillas to sell to zoos.

As logging companies cut down trees, they dig out roadways farther and farther into the rainforests. This makes it easier for other people to move on to the land and easier for hunters to get to the gorillas.

Who helps gorilla bands?

In the countries where gorillas live there are laws to protect them, but many people ignore these laws. Wars in these countries and a lack of **rangers** have meant that the laws have not been enforced.

Conservation groups work to protect gorillas and their **habitats.** For example, the United Nations has set up the Great Apes Survival Project (GRASP) to help all the **apes** of Africa. This project brings together wildlife groups from across the world to solve some of the gorillas' problems. The Dian Fossey Gorilla Fund is another organization that works to protect gorillas. It does things like educating people about gorillas and removing traps set by hunters.

Tourists who visit the gorillas can bring problems, such as human diseases. Also, gorillas can be frightened away by too much attention. However, tourism can be a good thing if it helps people to understand these animals so that they want to protect them.

Gorilla Facts

How many gorillas are left?

There are around 50,000 gorillas left in the wild. Of these, around 650 are mountain gorillas and 2,500 are eastern lowland gorillas. The rest—over 40,000—are western lowland gorillas. From these figures it is easy to see that the mountain gorilla is in greatest danger of **extinction**.

Making signs

In the 1970s a **female** gorilla called Koko learned to **communicate** with her keepers using sign language. Sign language is when people tell each other things by making signs and shapes with their hands. Since then, other gorillas have learned to do the same. When tested for intelligence, Koko scored between 70 and 95 on a scale where humans usually get 100!

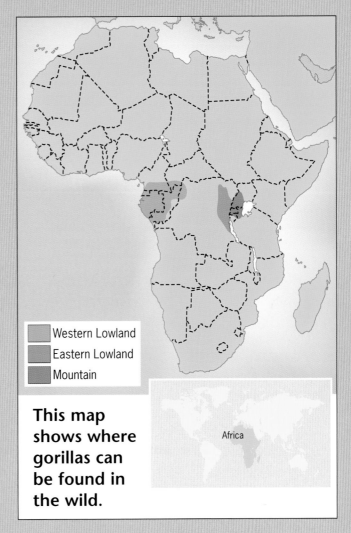

Western Lowland
Eastern Lowland
Mountain

Africa

This map shows where gorillas can be found in the wild.

Size and strength

A large **silverback** is about ten times stronger than the biggest human!

Noses and fingerprints

Each gorilla has its own unique nose, which means people can identify a gorilla by the distinct shape and pattern of wrinkles on its nose. Like humans, gorillas also have unique fingerprints.

Glossary

ape   tailless mammal that is closely related to humans. Gibbons, chimpanzees, and orangutans are kinds of apes.

canine   long, pointed tooth toward the front of an animal's mouth

communicate   pass on information

conservation   action to stop wild animals, plants, and places from dying out or being destroyed

digest   what an animal's body does to break down its food and take out what it needs to live and grow

display   put on a show of actions or movements that sends a message to another animal

dominant   leader of a group or most important member

extinct/extinction   when a species has died out and no longer exists

female   animal that, when grown up, can become a mother

groom/grooming   when one animal cleans bits of dirt, dead skin, or insect pests from the hair of another animal

habitat   where an animal or group of animals live

herbivore   animal that eats only or mainly plants and plant parts

home range   area within a habitat that a group of animals lives in

logger   person or company that chops down large numbers of trees and cuts them into logs to sell

male   animal that, when grown up, can become a father

mammal   one of a group of animals that includes humans. All mammals feed their babies milk from their own bodies and have some hair.

mate   produce young. After a male and female gorilla have mated, a baby begins to grow inside the female.

mineral   chemical found in rocks and soil. Animals need several different minerals to be healthy.

muscular   full of muscles. Muscles are parts of the body that help to make the bones and the rest of the body move.

nutrient   kind of chemical found in food that animals need to be healthy

pith   spongy white part beneath the outer layer of a plant part

predator   animal that hunts or catches other animals to eat

rainforest   forest of tall trees that grow in hot, wet places

ranger   person who patrols and guards the animals living in a particular area

rank   place in a scale or order of things. In an army, a major is a higher rank than an ordinary soldier.

silverback   large adult male gorilla that has silvery-gray hair on its back

social   live in a group

suckle/suckling   when a baby mammal drinks milk from its mother's body

termite   insect that lives in mud nests

whale   mammal that spends its life in water

More Books to Read

Dennard, Deborah. *Gorillas*. Chanhassen, Minn.: Creative
    Publishing, International, 2003.
Diamond, Claudia C. *Gorilla Families*. New York: The Rosen
    Publishing Group, Inc., 2002.
Hall, Margaret. *Gorillas and Their Infants*. Minnetonka, Minn.:
    Capstone Press, 2003.
Kendell, Patricia. *Gorillas*. Chicago: Raintree, 2003.
Milton, Joyce. *Gorillas*. New York: Random House, Inc., 2003.
Simon, Seymour. *Gorillas*. New York: HarperCollins, 2003.

Index